MODERN CURSIVE HANDWRITING

A Step-by-Step Guide and Workbook
to Learn Script Penmanship for Adults and Teens

with 150+ Practice Sheets and Bonus Free Downloads

MOLLY SUBER THORPE

Author of *Mastering Modern Calligraphy*

MODERN CURSIVE HANDWRITING:
A STEP-BY-STEP GUIDE AND WORKBOOK TO LEARN
SCRIPT PENMANSHIP FOR ADULTS AND TEENS

© 2022 by Molly Suber Thorpe.
Illustrations and lettering © 2022 by Molly Suber Thorpe.
All rights reserved.

Layout and cover design by Molly Suber Thorpe.

Digital typefaces:
Sagona by René Bieder
Proxima Nova by Mark Simonson

The designs and lettering in this volume are intended for personal
use of the reader and may be reproduced for that purpose only.

ISBN 979-8-9858650-3-5

First Edition: March 2022

Learn more about the author at:
mollysuberthorpe.com

This book belongs to

More books
BY MOLLY SUBER THORPE

Modern Cursive Handwriting Workbooks
Take Your New Cursive Skills to the Next Level with These Companion Workbooks

Trace-to-Learn Lettering Workbooks
A No-Frills Workbook Series for Different Hand Lettering Styles

Modern Calligraphy
Everything You Need to Know to Get Started in Script Calligraphy

Mastering Modern Calligraphy
Beyond the Basics: 2,700+ Pointed Pen Exemplars and Exercises for Developing Your Style

Decorative Alphabets
A Coloring Book of Letters and Borders

The Calligrapher's Business Handbook
Pricing and Policies for Lettering Artists

Table of Contents

Why Cursive?........................... 7
A Quick Note 11
Before You Begin 13
Free Downloads 15
Tools & Supplies 17
Position & Posture..................... 21
Speed & Slant 25
Letter & Guideline Anatomy 27
Warmup Drills 29
Lowercase Alphabet..................... 37
Uppercase Alphabet 69
Numbers & Symbols..................... 101
Letter Connections.................... 123
Common Words.......................... 141
Phrases & Paragraphs 159
Write A Letter........................ 171
Writing Prompts 185
Writing Guides........................ 193
Conclusion 201
About The Author 203

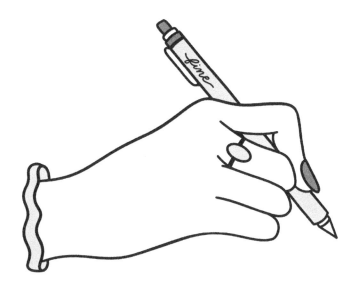

INTRODUCTION

Why Cursive?

There are many reasons to develop legible, consistent handwriting, some practical, others personal. This book will teach you the fundamentals of script penmanship through targeted exercises and in-depth explanations. I want you to find pleasure in writing by hand and take pride in how your handwriting looks — whether you have never tried cursive before, or are simply looking to improve your skill.

Handwriting helps us focus and remember things.

While most of us have now grown accustomed to composing thoughts in front of a screen, there is a focus brought about by good old-fashioned longhand. Whether it's taking notes for class or writing a to-do list, the tactile activity of putting pen to paper helps thoughts stick in our brain.

Handwriting requires both verbal and fine motor skills. It is also slower than typing. This combination of cognition, physical movement, and pace results in a greater processing of information *as we write it*, thereby increasing our retention and understanding. And scientific research backs this up. A 2014 study of college students found that the ones "who took notes on laptops performed worse on conceptual questions than students who took notes longhand."[1]

Can you read this letter written by my great-great-grandfather George in 1909? Give it a try, then turn the page to read the transcription.

Handwriting is relaxing.

And it's also inspiring! Sitting by oneself with just a pen and paper has a way of calming the mind and stirring our creativity. As a professional calligrapher, I make my living writing words beautifully, by hand, so my bias certainly shows here! However, in my years of teaching script writing to hundreds of students, I have seen the same effect time and time again. People are often surprised by the relaxing — even meditative — mood that freehand writing elicits.

Handwriting is personal.

It connects us to others more powerfully than the printed word. We all have people in our lives whose handwriting we recognize as instantly as their face. That's because it's personal. With the rise of texting and emails, handwritten notes and letters have fallen by the wayside. But a handwritten note will always feel more personal than a typed one — maybe now more than ever!

Handwriting is self-expression.

Nice handwriting also has a way of inspiring confidence. If you're embarrassed by your handwriting, you're less likely to spend much time doing it, or at least to take pleasure in it. But having handwriting you're proud of instills the confidence to write more, and to share that writing with others. (This applies to nice penmanship generally — not just cursive.)

Handwriting connects us to our past.

Finally, I would mention the connection between writing in cursive and understanding our past. I have a love for vintage manuscripts and historical documents. Were it not for my ability to *write* cursive fluently, it would be harder for me to *read* it. Letterforms and writing styles have evolved with time, but I'm still able to make out the words with relative ease because of my understanding of the fundamentals of script. Reading the handwritten words of my ancestors makes me feel closer to them.

---

[1]   Mueller, P. A. and Oppenheimer, D. M. (2014) 'The Pen Is Mightier Than the Keyboard: Advantages of Longhand Over Laptop Note Taking', *Psychological Science*, 25(6), pp. 1159–1168. https://doi.org/10.1177/0956797614524581

LETTER TRANSCRIPTION

Waseca Minn
Febry 23ᵈ 1909

Dear Mr. Thorpe,

    It is storming here today and as I am at the office I shall reply to your good letter of the 3ᵈ inst.* from here. I thank you most cordially for your kind invitation to make my home with you and Lilian and I shall always appreciate it but I assure you I have no thought of going on the retired list for the next fifteen years at least. I have many things I plan to do in the coming years (D.V.)** and it will brighten the years to know I have always a welcome awaiting me under your roof.

    Yes, my preference is a home in the Puget Sound Country and I hope the way will open for this although at present every thing seems pulling us here. With best wishes I am always

Faithfully Yours
Geo. J. Day

* "3rd instant" — the 3rd instance of the current month, in this case February 3rd
** "Deo Volente" — "God willing" in Latin

Practice the exercises in order.

For best results, **I recommend working through this book in order**. Take your time and remember to write slowly until you're confident with each letterform.

Consider tracing or photocopying the pages.

I designed this workbook with the intent that each exercise could be practiced over and over again. While you *can* write directly inside the book, I recommend that you trace the exemplars instead (see page 18), or photocopy the worksheets for personal use. This will extend the life of the book, so you can revisit each exercise as many times as you need.

Visit **mollysuberthorpe.com/cursive** to download free printable PDFs of blank lined paper and bonus practice sheets!

Lined paper is best for learning handwriting.

I designed the lined sheets in this workbook specifically for cursive handwriting. The ratio of uppercase to lowercase heights is in keeping with standard American cursive, and the spacing between lines is proportional to those heights.

However, **the height of the guideline spaces themselves are slightly larger than what everyday applications of cursive usually require**. I chose this size because it is the best letter height for learning. Medium-sized letters are easier to write slowly and deliberately — just what's needed when you're getting started. (So that you can practice smaller cursive writing, I've included an appendix of additional guideline sheets starting on page 193.)

And finally, perhaps most important of all: enjoy the process!

CHART YOUR PROGRESS!

Before starting your cursive practice, copy the quote below in your current handwriting. Come back to this page as you work your way through the book and repeat the exercise. Be sure to add the date to chart your progress over time!

You can make anything by writing.
— C. S. Lewis

___/___/___

___/___/___

___/___/___

TRY OUT DIFFERENT PENS AND PENCILS HERE

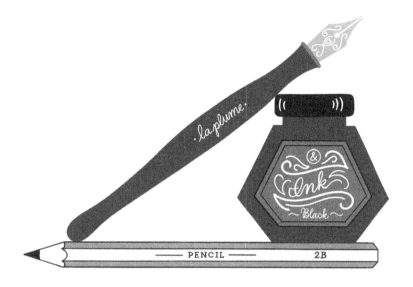

Tools & Supplies

The handwriting utensil you choose will make a big difference in your practice sessions. I recommend experimenting with different pens and pencils to find the ones that feel best in your hand and make writing the easiest.

PENCILS

Pencils have a unique way of gripping the paper that makes for smoother strokes. I recommend starting with a pencil if you're a beginner and want to focus more on the letter shapes than the tool itself. The softer the pencil, the easier the writing. A classic 2B pencil will work just fine, but I personally prefer mine softer, like 4B or 6B.

PENS

There are so many types of pens that the choice can feel overwhelming. Ballpoint, rollerball, gel, felt tip, fountain – the list goes on. Within each category are subcategories, ranging from point width to ink permanence.

When choosing a good pen for everyday handwriting, you should look for one with smooth, even ink flow. It shouldn't require much pressure to write, because greater pressure requires a tighter grip, which in turn leads to a sore hand! I also recommend a relatively fine tip, especially once you reach an intermediate level. For small handwriting, a fine point allows the letters' details to shine.

Rollerballs are my personal favorite handwriting pen because their water-based ink flows freely, requiring very little pressure to write. I usually reach for the Uni-Ball Eye Micro, which is smooth, opaque, fine-tipped, and fast-drying.

Ballpoint pens, while extremely popular, are not always a great choice if you're writing a lot, such as when taking notes. Their ink is oil-based, which means they don't dry out as fast as other pens, but it also means the ink can be viscous, requiring more pressure for a consistent ink flow.

Felt tip pens can be problematic because they tend to have wide points (although not always!) and their ink can bleed. And gel pens, while offering a great selection of vibrant colors, tend to have sticky ink that doesn't always flow in consistent lines.

Some people (myself included) love fountain pens for their flow and customizable nib flexibility. A good fountain pen loaded with fine ink is not only luxurious but can really improve the writing experience. If you're looking to get your first fountain pen but aren't ready to invest in a premium model, I recommend the Kaweko Classic Sport.

PAPER

The main factors to consider for handwriting practice paper are weight (i.e. how thick it is), texture (also known as "tooth"), and finish (i.e. the coating). Weight is important because paper that's too thin means your ink can bleed through to the other side, and the ink's moisture can cause the sheet to ripple and curl. A poor texture will cause some inks to bleed by absorbing it into the surrounding fibers. It will also cause your pen to snag or skip along the fibers and ridges. If the finish of the paper is too glossy, it will cause water-based inks to bead up, making smears and smudges almost inevitable.

Translucent paper can be used to trace letters and letter guidelines. Laserjet printer paper is an economical choice for this. For fancier tracing paper, I suggest layout bond or smooth vellum sheets. I prefer the brands Borden & Riley and Canson, respectively.

WRITING SURFACE

A slightly padded writing surface always yields nicer, smoother writing than a single sheet of paper on a hard surface. This is because if your pen can slightly press into the paper, it will grip the surface better, resulting in less shaky strokes. Writing directly in a notepad is great, but if you're writing on loose practice paper, put at least a couple more sheets under it. (The same applies to all writing, by the way — not just when you're learning. Writing a thank you note? Put some padding underneath. It will look better, I promise.)

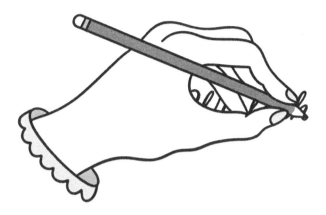

TIPS FOR LEFTIES

If you are left-handed, there are a few more considerations to take into account. In all likelihood, you have learned many ways to navigate writing as a lefty throughout your life, and already have pens and notebooks you prefer to use. Nonetheless, here are some tips that can improve your handwriting experience.

First, get a pen that is fast-drying and smudge resistant. With your hand moving left to right on the page, you're less likely to smear your ink if it dries quickly. Also be sure to select a pen with free-flowing ink. As stated above, I recommend this for everyone, but it's especially important for lefties so that when your pen is pushed across the paper (as opposed to pulled) it will not snag or skip.

When it comes to paper, instead of a left-bound notepad, you may prefer one with binding on the top, or simply to use loose practice sheets. Rhodia makes great top-bound notebooks with lined and dot grid pages.

FIND LINKS TO MY FAVORITE WRITING TOOLS AT

MOLLYSUBERTHORPE.COM/CURSIVE

Position and Posture

The way we hold our pen and sit at our desk can have a significant impact on our writing speed, legibility, and comfort.

HAND POSITIONS

While there are many ways to hold a pen, some are better than others, especially when writing for long periods of time. I cover the different grip types next, but regardless of which one you prefer, these two important principles always apply:

❧ Maintain a relaxed grip. Make sure you're extending your fingers, rather than scrunching them. (No white knuckles!) Your index finger should never be bent at greater than a ninety-degree angle.

❧ The end of your pen (or the eraser of your pencil) should ideally point toward your shoulder. For righties, this means the right shoulder, and for lefties, the left.

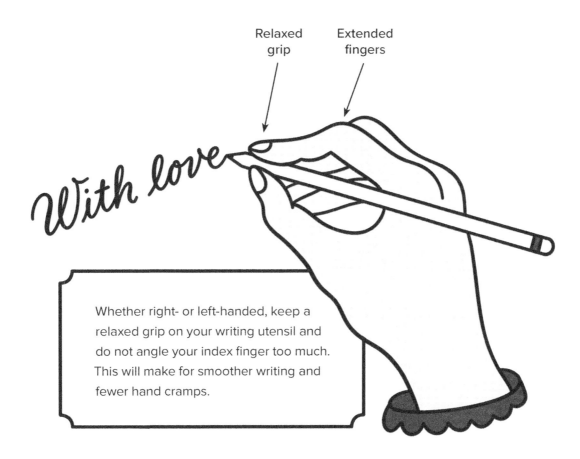

Whether right- or left-handed, keep a relaxed grip on your writing utensil and do not angle your index finger too much. This will make for smoother writing and fewer hand cramps.

PEN GRIPS

Below are the four most common pen grips. They describe both right- and left-handed positions. While all of these grips are acceptable, the first (dynamic tripod grip) is ideal for writing with ease because of the relaxed hand position and low pen angle.

For all of these grips, only the outer edge of your hand (pinky side) should be resting on the paper. Your pinky itself will always touch the paper, but depending on how much you curl your fourth finger, it may touch as well.

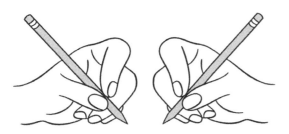

DYNAMIC TRIPOD GRIP

This is the most common grip and is ideal for writing with ease. Three fingers touch the pen – hence the name 'tripod' – stabilizing it between the middle finger's knuckle, index finger, and thumb. The fourth finger and pinky curl under the hand.

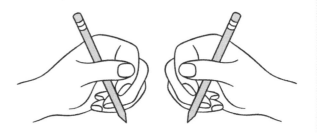

LATERAL TRIPOD GRIP

Three fingers touch the pen but this differs from a dynamic tripod grip because the thumb extends over the pen and touches the index finger. This creates a steeper angle of the pen and may lead to hand cramps after long stretches of writing.

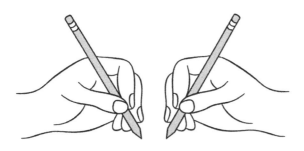

DYNAMIC QUADRUPOD GRIP

Four fingers touch the pen – hence the name 'quadrupod'. Unlike a tripod grip, the middle finger also rests on the pen, with the fourth finger providing stability from behind. The pinky curls under and the pen angle is steeper than with dynamic tripod.

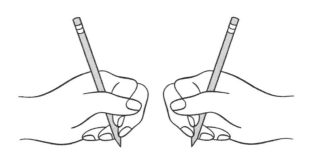

LATERAL QUADRUPOD GRIP

Four fingers still touch the pen but this differs from a dynamic quadrupod grip because the thumb extends over the pen and touches the index finger. This creates a much steeper pen angle and may lead to hand cramps after long stretches of writing.

PAPER ANGLE

The angle of your paper or notebook in front of you plays a role in how comfortably you can write, the ease with which your pen can move across the page, and the italic slant of your letters.

A general rule of thumb is that the lines of your paper should be roughly perpendicular to your forearm. This isn't an exact science, but it's a good starting point to find the best paper angle for you. If you find that your elbow is squeezed up against your side, or that your letters are more cramped at the beginning of a line, adjust your paper's angle slightly away from you. You might be surprised by just how big a difference this can make!

Another handy tip is to move your paper away from you as you write, rather than move your arm backward with each line. This keeps your arm stabilized on the table.

These are the most common hand positions and paper angles for left- and right-handed people.

SITTING POSTURE

The goal of good writing posture is to sit over your paper, minimizing how much you're leaning forward. Your eyes should be directly over your paper, and your forearm should be just gently skimming the table. Achieve this with a sturdy desk chair without wheels. Sit toward the edge of your seat so that your thighs are mostly off the chair and your feet touch the ground. This position should allow your eyes to be directly over the paper without craning your neck.

If you'll be writing for a long time, try moving the foot that corresponds to your writing hand side slightly forward, so that more weight is on it, taking some stress off your core. If your feet can't touch the ground even when you're at the edge of your seat, use a foot rest to maintain a steady posture.

Keep your elbow off the edge of the table, resting just your forearm on it. Your arm should be able to glide across the writing surface, so do not anchor it so firmly that you feel a strain in your shoulder. Also, avoid leaning your body against the table because that can inhibit arm movement.

COMMON GRIP AND POSTURE ISSUES

➤ My hand is cramped, even when I keep a loose grip.

Make sure you're extending your fingers, rather than scrunching them. Also check that only the outer edge of your hand (pinky side) is resting on the paper.

If the above adjustments don't fix the issue, try adding a pen grip that widens the pen barrel, or getting a fatter pen. You won't have to grip it as hard, which will keep your lines smoother and your hand more relaxed. Many people with arthritis also find this solution helpful.

Lefties may find that a triangular-shaped pencil helps. These special pencils can be found in most art stores, and they're specifically designed to promote the most ergonomic grip for a left hand.

➤ I'm clenching my pen too tightly, no matter how hard I try to relax!

There's a funny trick for this that calligraphers often use. Squeeze something, like an eraser or a tennis ball, in your non-writing hand. It's hard to maintain a tight grip with both hands at once, so eventually your writing hand's grip should loosen.

➤ My shoulder and arm get tight after a while.

First, check your pen grip and the tricks above. A tight arm could simply be an extension of a tight writing hand. However, it's also possible that you're holding your arm too close to your body, keeping your shoulder static. Try moving your paper a little farther away from your body, and angling it slightly more than you're used to. (For righties, that means angling it counter-clockwise, and for lefties, clockwise.)

➤ My neck and back hurt!

This is likely the result of leaning too far over your paper. Make sure you're not sitting too far back in your chair and that both feet are touching the floor.

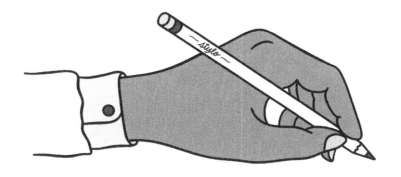

Speed and Slant

WRITING SPEED

As you make your way through the exercises in this book, write very, very slowly at first. You're training yourself in new hand-eye coordination! Even if your brain knows how you want the letters to look, your hand hasn't been programmed with all the necessary signals yet. **Trace the letterforms very slowly, then draw them freehand at the same speed.** Only once you are able to draw a letter with smooth, controlled strokes should you increase your writing speed.

ITALIC SLANT

Cursive is normally written at a slant, however the precise angle is not set in stone. In fact, many cursive programs teach an entirely upright writing style, akin to printed handwriting. Still, a slight forward slant – no matter how slight – is traditional.

The italic slant can vary dramatically from one person to the next, though, and ultimately comes down to personal style and preference. (If you're familiar with calligraphy, you will know that certain calligraphic styles have rigidly-defined italic slants. This is not the case for American cursive.)

The cursive taught in this book has a twenty-degree slant. This is common handwriting italicization. However, you will notice that I do not include italic guidelines for you to follow. This is because italic slant is not a crucial consideration while learning cursive letterforms. Ultimately, as your handwriting style evolves and becomes your own, your slant will settle into one that you're comfortable with based on how you hold your pen and angle your paper.

If you want to practice with some slanted guidelines, I've included various options in the guideline appendix at the end of this book.

TERMINOLOGY

ASCENDER: The vertical portion of a lowercase letter that extends above the x-height to the ascender line.

ASCENDER LINE: The line up to which an ascender extends.

BASELINE: The line upon which letters sit. Descenders fall below the baseline.

BOWL: The rounded stroke enclosing a counter.

CAP HEIGHT: The height of a capital letter, starting from the baseline. In styles where ascenders are the same height as capitals, the ascender line and cap height line are the same. That is not always the case, but it is for the cursive style taught in this book.

CONNECTOR STROKE: A stroke that exits one letter and enters the next.

COUNTER: An enclosed space within a letter, such as in D and d.

CROSSBAR: A horizontal stroke in a letter, as in A and t.

DESCENDER: The vertical portion of a lowercase letter that extends below the baseline to the descender line.

DESCENDER LINE: The line down to which a descender extends.

ENTRY STROKE: The stroke leading into a letter at the beginning of a word.

EXIT STROKE: The stroke at the end of a word coming out of the last letter.

EYE: The counter of a lowercase e.

GUIDELINES: A layout of lines that helps you write with an even baseline and letter proportions. While usually horizontal, guidelines can also be slanted or curved.

LOOP: An enclosed bowl which is part of a script letter's ascender or descender, as in b, g, and l.

MAJUSCULE: Uppercase letter (a.k.a. capital letter).

MINUSCULE: Lowercase letter.

OVERTURN: A curved stroke that moves up and then turns downward when it reaches the waistline, as in lowercase m.

SHOULDER: The curved hump of a letter, as in n and cursive r.

STEM: A letter's vertical downstroke(s). The letter t has one, h has two, and m has three.

TITTLE: The dot of an i or j; likely from combining the words 'tiny' and 'little'.

UNDERTURN: A curved stroke that moves down and then turns upward when it reaches the baseline, as in lowercase u.

WAISTLINE: The line at the top of a lettering style's x-height space (a.k.a. the meanline).

X-HEIGHT: The space between the baseline and waistline, named for the height of a lowercase x. All letters occupy the x-height space, and lowercase letters without ascenders or descenders occupy *only* this space (examples: a, m, o, x).

Letter Anatomy

Understanding the components of letterforms, how they connect, and the lines they adhere to will guide you in your practice.

Your Turn!

Can you identify the letter anatomy and various guidelines?

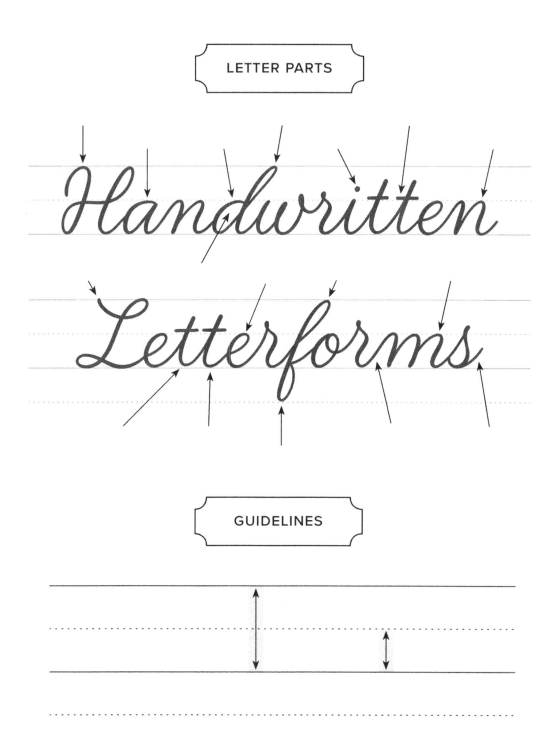

Warmup Drills

GET YOUR HAND MOVING

In these warmup exercises, you will practice common cursive strokes on their own, before combining them into letters in the following sections.

All script writing follows a simple rhythm of upward pen movement (upstrokes) followed by downward pen movement (downstrokes). These warmup drills will get your hand accustomed to the correct up-down strokes, in preparation for letters themselves.

As a beginner, it is best to do some warmup exercises each time you sit down to practice your cursive. Once this writing style becomes second nature, you won't have to do them every time, but you could revisit them if you ever find yourself rusty or stiff.

Use scrap paper for this when you run out of space in this book. Warmups don't have to look pretty!

Start writing at the dot and follow the arrow directions.
Write each character without lifting your pen.

DOWNSTROKES: Starting at the top, draw down to the left.

UPSTROKES: Starting at the bottom, draw up to the right.

UNDERTURNS: This down-up curve is the rounded part of the letter u.

OVERTURNS: This up-down curve is the rounded part of the letter n.

UNDER-OVER TURNS: Combine under- and overturns into one fluid stroke.

OVER-OVER-UNDER TURNS: Connect two overlapping overturns followed by an underturn.

DOUBLE UNDER TURNS: Starting with an upstroke, draw two overlapping underturns.

OVALS: These simple ellipses start at the top and move counter-clockwise.

'e' LOOP: Draw short, connected loops without lifting your pen.

'l' LOOP: Draw tall, connected loops without lifting your pen. Then write some connected 'ele' loops.

'h' LOOP: These tall loops with straight downstrokes are the basis of letters h and k.

WARMUP DRILLS

w w

o o o o

e e e

l l l

e l e

f f f

Keep going!

Use this space for future warmup exercises.

Lowercase Alphabet

In the following pages, you will learn the lowercase cursive alphabet. Take your time to trace the letters slowly and carefully, then practice them freehand in the remaining space.

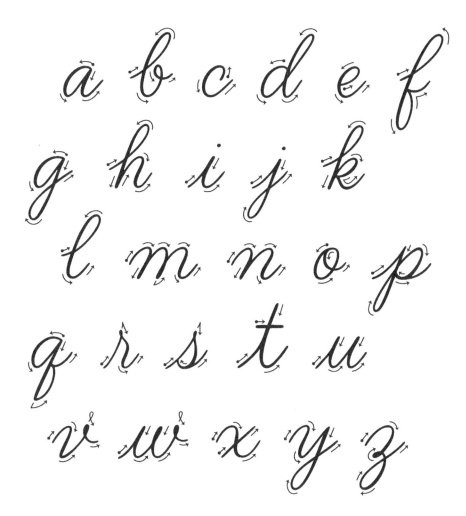

LOWERCASE ALPHABET

A NOTE ON STYLE

As you learned in the Letter Anatomy section (p. 27), entry strokes lead into a letter. For some letters, like **a** and **g**, an entry stroke at the beginning of a word is entirely optional because it is not essential to the letter's structure. For others, like **b** and **h**, it is hard to remove the entry stroke without affecting the integrity of the letter, so an entry stroke is always used. Whether you use an entry stroke when it's not essential is entirely a matter of stylistic preference. In these individual letter practice pages, I do not include non-essential entry strokes.

Start writing at the dot and follow the arrow directions. Write each character without lifting your pen. The only exceptions are those that have numbers next to the arrows, indicating the order in which to write multiple strokes.

a a a a a a a a a a a a a

a

a

a

a

b b b b b b b b b b b b

b

b

b

b

b

LOWERCASE ALPHABET

a
b

a
b

a
b

a
b

a
b

a
b

a
b

c

c c c c c c c c c c c c

d

d d d d d d d d d d d

LOWERCASE ALPHABET

c
d
c
d
c
d
c
d
c
d
c
d
c
d

LOWERCASE ALPHABET

e

f

e

f

e

f

e

f

e

f

e

f

g

h

LOWERCASE ALPHABET

LOWERCASE ALPHABET

i

j

i

j

i

j

i

j

i

j

i

j

LOWERCASE ALPHABET

k
l
k
l
k
l
k
l
k
l
k
l
k
l

m

m m m m m m m m m

n

n n n n n n n n n

LOWERCASE ALPHABET

m

n

m

n

m

n

m

n

m

n

m

n

m

n

LOWERCASE ALPHABET

o

p

o

p

o

p

o

p

o

p

o

p

o

p

LOWERCASE ALPHABET

q
r
q
r
q
r
q
r
q
r
q
r
q
r

LOWERCASE ALPHABET

s

t

s

t

s

t

s

t

s

t

s

t

s

t

u

v

u

v

u

v

u

v

u

v

u

v

u

v

LOWERCASE ALPHABET

w

x

w

x

w

x

w

x

w

x

w

x

w

x

LOWERCASE ALPHABET

y

z

y

z

y

z

y

z

y

z

y

z

y

z

Come back to this page in a few days to test your lowercase letters freehand.

Uppercase Alphabet

In the following pages, you will learn the uppercase cursive alphabet. Take your time to trace the letters slowly and carefully, then practice them freehand in the remaining space.

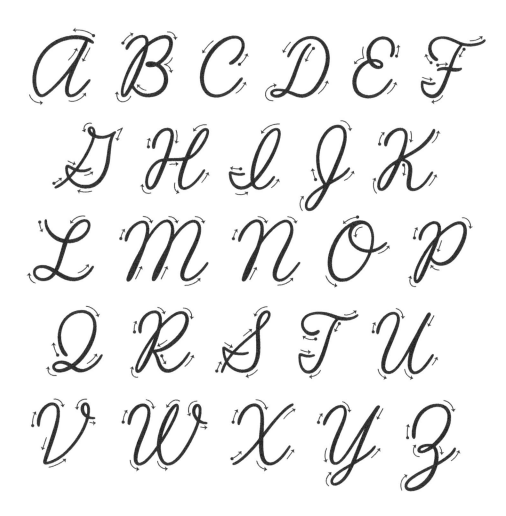

UPPERCASE ALPHABET 67

Start writing at the dot and follow the arrow directions. Write each character without lifting your pen. The only exceptions are those that have numbers next to the arrows, indicating the order in which to write multiple strokes.

UPPERCASE ALPHABET

UPPERCASE ALPHABET

C

D

C

D

C

D

C

D

C

D

C

D

C

D

UPPERCASE ALPHABET

UPPERCASE ALPHABET

G

H

G

H

G

H

G

H

G

H

G

H

G

H

UPPERCASE ALPHABET

𝒦 𝒦 𝒦 𝒦 𝒦 𝒦 𝒦 𝒦 𝒦 𝒦

ℒ ℒ ℒ ℒ ℒ ℒ ℒ ℒ ℒ ℒ

m m m m m m m
n n n n n n n

UPPERCASE ALPHABET

m
n
m
n
m
n
m
n
m
n
m
n

UPPERCASE ALPHABET 83

UPPERCASE ALPHABET

UPPERCASE ALPHABET

UPPERCASE ALPHABET

UPPERCASE ALPHABET

W
X
W
X
W
X
W
X
W
X
W
X
W
X

UPPERCASE ALPHABET

Y
z
Y
z
Y
z
Y
z
Y
z
Y
z
Y
z

COMPLETE ALPHABET REVIEW

A B C D E F G H I
J K L M N O P Q R
S T U V W X Y Z

A B C D E F G H I
J K L M N O P Q R
S T U V W X Y Z

Aa Bb Cc Dd Ee Ff Gg

Hh Ii Jj Kk Ll Mm

Nn Oo Pp Qq Rr Ss Tt

Uu Vv Ww Xx Yy Zz

Aa Bb Cc Dd Ee Ff Gg

Hh Ii Jj Kk Ll Mm

Nn Oo Pp Qq Rr Ss Tt

Uu Vv Ww Xx Yy Zz

Aa Bb Cc Dd Ee Ff Gg

Hh Ii Jj Kk Ll Mm

Nn Oo Pp Qq Rr Ss Tt

Uu Vv Ww Xx Yy Zz

Aa Bb Cc Dd Ee Ff Gg
Hh Ii Jj Kk Ll Mm
Nn Oo Pp Qq Rr Ss Tt
Uu Vv Ww Xx Yy Zz

UPPERCASE ALPHABET

Numbers and Symbols

In the following pages, you will learn cursive numbers and some commonly-used symbols. Take your time to trace them slowly and carefully, then practice them freehand in the remaining space.

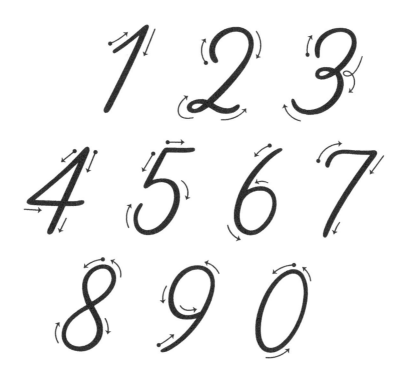

NUMBERS & SYMBOLS 99

Start writing at the dot and follow the arrow directions. Write each character without lifting your pen. The only exceptions are those that have numbers next to the arrows, indicating the order in which to write multiple strokes.

NUMBERS & SYMBOLS

NUMBERS & SYMBOLS

5 5555555555

6 6666666666

NUMBERS & SYMBOLS

NUMBERS & SYMBOLS

NUMBERS & SYMBOLS

1 2 3 4 5 6 7 8 9 0

1 2 3 4 5 6 7 8 9 0

1 2 3 4 5 6 7 8 9 0

zero *zero zero*

one *one one*

two *two two*

three *three three*

four four four

five five five

six six six

seven seven seven

eight eight eight

nine nine nine

ten ten ten

NUMBERS & SYMBOLS

NUMBERS & SYMBOLS

# # # # # # # # # #

#

#

#

#

#

0 0 0 0 0 0 0 0 0 0

0

0

0

0

0

NUMBERS & SYMBOLS

NUMBER AND SYMBOL REVIEW

(zero) (three) (six) (nine)

eight?? 782?! zero!! 5!

3 & 4   ten & two   one & five

#two   #four   #seven   #ten

@eight   @three   five@six

18   27   36   45

142   358   607

20486   79315

Letter Connections

Connected letterforms are the defining characteristic of cursive penmanship. By design, one rarely needs to lift their pen when writing cursive words, which means that the connector strokes between letters are nearly as important as the letters themselves.

The following sections cover how lowercase letters connect to each other, and how uppercase letters connect to lowercase ones.

Lowercase Letter Connections

While connecting one letter to the next is often intuitive, there are strokes and techniques that make connected script more efficient and elegant.

I categorize the lowercase script alphabet into five groups based on related structures and connector strokes. When two letters connect, the first letter's *exit stroke* becomes the next letter's *entry stroke*, hence the two in combination become a single *connector stroke*.

CONNECTOR STROKES

What follows is a detailed breakdown of each group so you can understand their commonalities and see how they connect. After you have gained an understanding of these letter relationships, you will practice common lowercase letter pairs yourself in the pages that follow.

LOWERCASE GROUP ONE

These fourteen letters form a group because they connect simply and intuitively. Just one fluid stroke is required to connect any two of these letters. No adjustments need be made to the letters' shapes to accommodate the connection.

f h i j k l m n p t u x y z

Here are examples of Group One connector strokes:

plum tux limit flip

LOWERCASE GROUP TWO

The seemingly simple letter **e** gets a group of its own because of a minor – yet crucial – adjustment to connector strokes that lead into it.

e

In order to create the correct shape of an **e**'s eye, the angle of the entry stroke must change direction midway. Instead of a simple, fluid stroke, **e** connectors bend in the middle, moving slightly more to the right before curving upward again:

e   be   ce   ee   fe

Here are examples of **e** connections in various words:

peel   mere   yet   axe

LOWERCASE GROUP THREE

These five form a group because of the shared curve shape on the left side. To avoid lifting one's pen when drawing these letters, a small portion at the top of these letters' bowls gets drawn over twice.

a c d g q

In the examples below, you can see that the connector strokes curve up and over the top curves. Completing the letters then requires doubling back on the top portion of the curve – moving to the left and down to draw the bowl shape.

ma   uc   nd   rg   eq

aqua   flag   ice   end

LOWERCASE GROUP FOUR

These four letters are distinguished by their exit strokes, which end near the *waistline*, rather than the baseline. This means that when you finish writing any of these letters, your pen will be closer to the top of the next letter than the bottom.

b o v w

This does not impact connector strokes that enter *into* these letters, however, letters that come *after* them sometimes need to be adjusted. These are examples of Group Four letters connecting to one another:

vov wow boo

These examples show Group Four letters combined with the previous three Groups:

bill oak even who

LOWERCASE GROUP FIVE

Letters **r** and **s** rely heavily on their entry strokes for their structure. Since their entry strokes start at the baseline, these two letters must be adjusted the most to accommodate the letters in Group Four.

r s

These examples show how Group Four letters connect to **r** and **s**:

br bs or os vr vs wr ws

Here you can compare the connector strokes of **r** and **s** when preceded by letters in Groups One, Two, and Three, versus Group Four:

irks cruise brew crack

ab ab ab

ac ac ac

be be be

bo bo bo

br br br

bs bs bs

ea ea ea

e e e e ee ee

er er er

ex ex ex

fa fa fa

fe fe fe

ff ff ff

fr fr fr

LETTER CONNECTIONS

go go go

gr gr gr

ha ha ha

he he he

hy hy hy

ir ir ir

ka ka ka

ke ke ke

ll ll ll

ly ly ly

mm mm mm

mo mo mo

ms ms ms

nn nn nn

LETTER CONNECTIONS

no no no

oa oa oa

of of of

oo oo oo

or or or

os os os

ou ou ou

pp pp pp

pr pr pr

qu qu qu

re re re

rr rr rr

rs rs rs

sc sc sc

LETTER CONNECTIONS

ss ss ss

st st st

th th th

tt tt tt

va va va

ve ve ve

vo vo vo

vr vr vr

vs vs vs

we we we

wh wh wh

wr wr wr

ws ws ws

zy zy zy

Uppercase Letter Connections

Most uppercase letters — but not all — can be connected to a lowercase letter.

These letters *can* connect to a lowercase because they end on or near the baseline:

A B C E G H I J K L
M N O* Q R S U X Y Z

* *Note that the exit stroke of this O extends lower than usual. This is a minor adjustment you should make to O when connecting it to a lowercase letter.*

These letters *cannot* connect because they don't have exit strokes near the baseline:

D F P T* V W

* *There is one optional exception for uppercase T: the letter combination Th, which appears later in this chapter. For the most part, though, T remains disconnected.*

To build on the lowercase connection practice in the previous section, this section includes full words instead of just letter pairs.

Amuse

Belong

LETTER CONNECTIONS

Create *Create*

Enrich *Enrich*

Grow *Grow*

Hope *Hope*

Imagine *Imagine*

Join *Join*

Know *Know*

Learn *Learn*

Marvel *Marvel*

Notice *Notice*

*Opine *Opine*

Question *Question*

Reveal *Reveal*

Study *Study*

Here is the way to connect T with h:

Think Think

It's perfectly fine to leave them disconnected, too:

Think Think

Unite Unite

Xerox Xerox

Yearn Yearn

Zoom Zoom

* Remember that when connecting uppercase O to a lowercase letter, you should adjust the final stroke so that it exits closer to the baseline:

Common Words

In the following pages, you will practice the 98 most common words in English that have two or more letters. (The words 'a' and 'I' round off the top 100 list, but you already know how to write them!)

Following that list are the colors of the rainbow, with uppercase first letters for additional upper-lower combination practice.

about *about about*

all *all all*

also *also also*

and *and and*

as *as as*

at *at at*

be *be be*

because *because because*

but *but but*

by *by by*

can *can can*

come *come come*

could *could could*

day *day day*

do *do do*

even *even even*

find *find find*

first *first first*

for *for for*

from *from from*

get *get get*

give *give give*

go *go go*

have *have have*

he *he he*

her *her her*

here *here here*

him *him him*

COMMON WORDS

his his his

how how how

if if if

in in in

into into into

it it it

its its its

just *just just*

know *know know*

like *like like*

look *look look*

make *make make*

man *man man*

many *many many*

me *me me*

more *more more*

my *my my*

new *new new*

no *no no*

not *not not*

now *now now*

of *of of*

on *on on*

one *one one*

only *only only*

or *or or*

other *other other*

our *our our*

COMMON WORDS

out

people

say

see

she

so

some

take *take take*

tell *tell tell*

than *than than*

that *that that*

the *the the*

their *their their*

them *them them*

then *then then*

there *there there*

these *these these*

they *they they*

thing *thing thing*

think *think think*

this *this this*

those *those those*

time *time time*

to *to to*

two *two two*

up *up up*

use *use use*

very *very very*

want *want want*

way *way way*

we *we we*

well *well well*

what *what what*

when *when when*

which *which which*

who *who who*

will *will will*

with *with with*

would *would would*

year *year year*

yes *yes yes*

you *you you*

Colors

Red

Orange

Yellow

Green

Blue

Violet

Purple

Pink

Black

White

Gray

Gold

Silver

Phrases and Paragraphs

With common words under your belt — and lots of practice connecting letters — it's time to string words together into sentences. This chapter covers popular expressions and greetings, pangrams, and short quotations.

The primary goals here are to practice word spacing and the addition of punctuation.

Expressions & Greetings

These expressions are commonly used in letters and greeting cards.
The next chapter continues this theme, and is all about letter-writing!

I love you

Happy Birthday!

Congratulations!

Get well soon

Thinking of you...

Happy Holidays

Happy Thanksgiving

Season's Greetings

Merry Christmas

Happy Hanukkah

Happy New Year

Be My Valentine

Happy Halloween

Pangrams

Pangrams are sentences that use every letter of the alphabet, making them especially helpful for practicing handwriting.

The quick brown fox jumps over a lazy dog.

Sphinx of black quartz, judge my vow.

The five boxing wizards jumped quickly.

My girl wove six dozen plaid jackets before she quit.

How vexingly quick daft zebras jump!

Brown jars prevented the mixture from freezing too quickly.

Quotations

What better topic for practicing writing than that of writing itself?

Writing comes from reading and reading is the finest teacher of how to write. ~Annie Proulx

There is something delicious about writing the first words of a story. ~Beatrix Potter

Let me live, love, and say it well in good sentences.
      ~Sylvia Plath

I write to discover what I know. ~Flannery O'Connor

Dreams are necessary to life. ~Anaïs Nin

If there's a book that you want to read, but it hasn't been written yet, then you must write it.
~Toni Morrison

Write what should not be forgotten. ~Isabel Allende

Writing is the geometry of the soul. ~ Plato

You can make anything by writing. ~ C. S. Lewis

Writers do not merely reflect and interpret life, they inform and shape life. ~ E. B. White

In the black ink of my poetry, the one I love may still shine bright. ~William Shakespeare

I love the smell of book ink in the morning. ~Umberto Eco

Always be a poet, even in prose. ~Charles Baudelaire

Write A Letter

PUT YOUR NEW SKILLS TO PRACTICAL USE

In today's digital world, snail mail letters and envelope addressing are two of the most common applications of longhand. Indeed, they are a driving force behind the resurgence of cursive and calligraphy in recent years. As such, no book about penmanship would be complete without letter-writing practice.

The pages that follow cover useful vocabulary for written correspondence, envelope addressing etiquette, and templates for writing your own missives.

Letter-Addressing Vocabulary

Dear

Hello

Greetings!

Mr. Mrs.

Ms. Miss

To whom it may concern

Sincerely,

Love,

Thank you,

Yours truly,

Best wishes,

Kind regards,

From:

Avenue Ave.

Boulevard Blvd.

Drive Dr.

Road Rd.

Street St.

Apartment Apt. No.

Suite Ste.

Dates & Days

January

February

March

April

May

June

July

August

September

October

November

December

2024 2025 2026 2027

Monday

Tuesday

Wednesday

Thursday

Friday

Saturday

Sunday

Envelope Addressing Conventions

As a professional calligrapher who has addressed thousands of invitations in my career, I'm frequently asked about envelope etiquette, such as how to address a married couple when the wife kept her maiden name. While there are a number of traditional conventions for addressing envelopes, this is the twenty-first century and Emily Post won't be looking over your shoulder!

So my advice? **Follow conventions that will make both you and your guests feel comfortable**. This may mean adhering to tradition, or it may mean disregarding these conventions entirely in favor of an informal or creative approach. If you're sending a batch of invitations and you know some guests would prefer titles and others wouldn't, nothing should stop you from mixing it up.

Here are the most common envelope addressing conventions:

ADDRESSEE	CONVENTION	EXAMPLE
Single woman – young and unmarried	Miss	Miss Marly Stewart
Single woman – older or with undisclosed marital status	Ms.	Ms. Eloise Sanchez
Single man	Mr.	Mr. Vasileios Spyros
Married couple – man and woman with same last name	Mr. and Mrs.	Mr. and Mrs. Stephan McGregor
Married couple – man and woman who kept her maiden name	Ms. and Mr.	Ms. Cat Bartosz and Mr. Virgil Bennet
Married couple – women	Mrs. and Mrs.	Mrs. Olga Abbas and Mrs. Nadia Silje
Married couple – men	Mr. and Mr.	Mr. Hui Chu and Mr. Jacob Cornett
Unmarried couple living together	Two lines; no "and"	Mr. Daniel Vardanyan Miss/Ms. Flora Bancroft
Religious leader	Unabbreviated title	Rabbi [and Mrs.] David Behr
Member of the military	Unabbreviated title	Colonel Christina Mooney

Write a letter...

(If you need an idea, thank you notes are always a good choice!)

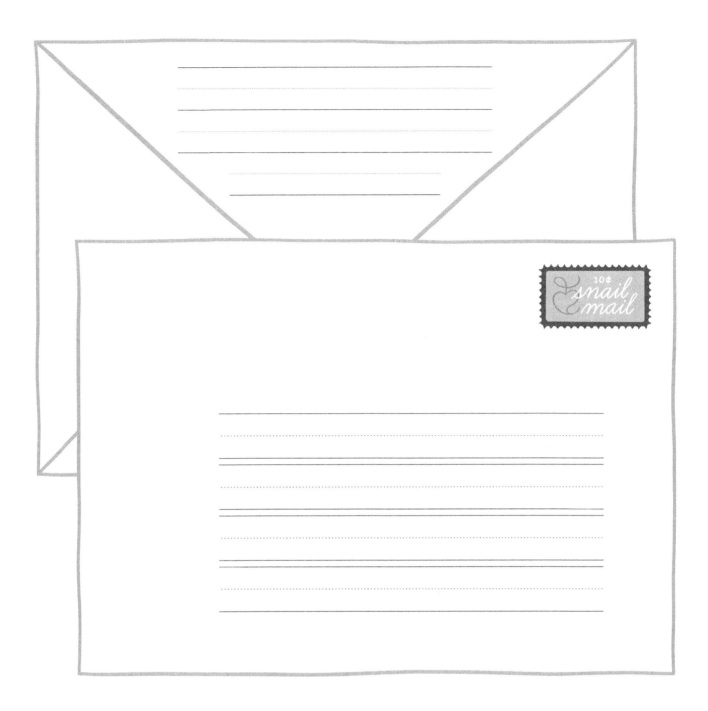

...and address the envelope.

DOWNLOAD THESE PRINTABLE ENVELOPE TEMPLATES:
MOLLYSUBERTHORPE.COM/CURSIVE

WRITE A LETTER

Writing Prompts

MORE FREEHAND PRACTICE

Don't let writer's block get in the way of your practice! If your mind goes blank as soon as you try to think of something to write, then you're not alone. (It happens to me all the time!)

Here are some prompts to keep you going. But when in doubt, to-do lists and diary entries are always a great choice.

What's your favorite line from a book or movie?

What's a joke that always makes you laugh?

Describe your favorite restaurant.

Describe your ideal vacation.

What did you do yesterday?

What will you do tomorrow?

Keep Going!

PRACTICE PROMPTS & IDEAS

Keep improving your new handwriting skills with daily practice. Below are some more ideas for handwriting projects, but when in doubt, lists and diary entries are excellent go-to exercises!

Handwriting exercises and projects:

- A letter of thanks to your favorite teacher
- Your favorite song lyrics
- A love note on fine stationery
- Sticker labels for your kitchen pantry
- Captions in a family photo album
- A letter to your state or local representative
- A daily journal entry
- A new design of your personal signature

Writing Guides

CUT OUT, TRACE, PHOTOCOPY, PRINT

After a lot of practice, you will be able to write beautifully without lines, but they are absolutely necessary while you're learning. (Even professional calligraphers use guidelines when we work!)

Everyday applications of cursive often require smaller writing than what is taught in the work pages of this book. So now that you have mastered cursive letters and words at medium size, it's time to experiment with the height and line spacing of your writing.

The pages that follow provide a variety of blank writing guide sheets. The x-heights vary from medium to very small, and some have slant lines to help you practice a uniform italic slant.

The first guide sheet ("Medium Letters") is the one used in this book.

You will notice dashed lines to make it easy to cut out these pages. I recommend that you reuse these sheets again and again by either photocopying them or placing tracing paper on top. You can also **download free printable versions at mollysuberthorpe.com/cursive**.

MEDIUM LETTERS • BEGINNER

SMALL LETTERS • INTERMEDIATE

SMALL LETTERS WITH ITALIC LINES • ADVANCED

Congratulations!

Congratulations on completing this workbook! I hope you've kindled a love of cursive that you will continue to develop into a lifelong habit.

This book's exercises covered the fundamentals of cursive, getting you accustomed to the letterforms and movements. But remember: handwriting is very personal. Ultimately you should embrace your own, unique style. If you see letter adjustments emerging in your writing that you like, incorporate them! If you feel your style is becoming less legible, return to this workbook to refresh yourself on the fundamentals.

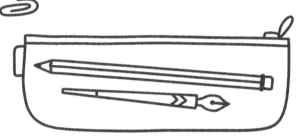

Share your progress on Instagram with the tag:
#SHAREMYSCRIPT

Tag me so I can have a peek:
@MOLLYSUBERTHORPE

About the Author

Molly Suber Thorpe creates custom lettering for brands and individuals around the world, digital assets for artists, and bestselling books for calligraphers. Since 2009, she has empowered aspiring letterers to refine their skills through her books, classes, and tools, helping them unlock new creative opportunities and launch successful careers.

Molly is recognized as a pioneering influence in the modern calligraphy movement, being one of the first calligraphers to embrace the whimsical pointed pen styles and bold color palettes that have become so popular today.

She has collaborated with clients including Google Arts & Culture, Michael Kors, Martha Stewart, Lonely Planet, Fendi, and more. Her work and words have been featured in such publications as The Guardian, The Wall Street Journal, Martha Stewart Weddings, Los Angeles Times, and Buzzfeed.

Molly also loves to teach. Along with offering in-person calligraphy workshops in the United States and Europe, she is recognized as a Skillshare Top Teacher, with her courses amassing over 2 million minutes of view time and reaching more than 45,000 students.

In 2016, Molly launched Calligrafile.com, a free resource hub for calligraphers, lettering artists, type enthusiasts, and creative freelancers. As the largest website of its kind, it features contributions from over two dozen artists and serves thousands of users worldwide.

The TRACE-TO-LEARN LETTERING Series

Want to learn more styles of hand lettering?

Trace-to-Learn Lettering is a no-frills workbook series for learning styles from brush script to flourished calligraphy.

PENMANSHIP PRACTICE FOR BEGINNERS AND BEYOND

THE MODERN CURSIVE HANDWRITING WORKBOOK SERIES

Continue improving your penmanship!

Practice the cursive skills you learned here in *Modern Cursive Handwriting* with the companion workbooks.

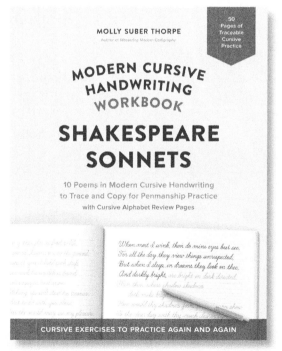

SEE ALL MY BOOKS AT
MOLLYSUBERTHORPE.COM/BOOKS

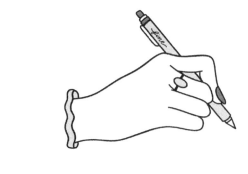

SITE
mollysuberthorpe.com

BLOG
mollysuberthorpe.com/news

INSTAGRAM
@mollysuberthorpe

YOUTUBE
MollySuberThorpeLetters

FREE LETTERING TOOLKIT
mollysletteringtoolkit.com

Made in the USA
Las Vegas, NV
15 November 2024